with/holding

Caitlin Press Inc.
3375 Ponderosa Way,
Qualicum Beach, BC V9K 2J8
www.caitlin-press.com

Typeset by Vici Johnstone
Edited by Chelene Knight
Images on pages 8,22,34-37,57,140,161,171 were rendered by Andrew Hawryshkewich

Cover image: Digitally altered photo from Dangling Modifiers, 2019, mixed media video installation by Chantal Gibson (artist) and Adrian Bisek (videographer).

Epigraphs on pages 97 and 146 from Teaching to Transgress: Education as the Practice of Freedom, bell hooks, © 1994, Routledge. Reproduced by permission of Taylor & Francis Group.

Printed in Canada

Caitlin Press Inc. acknowledges financial support from the Government of Canada and the Canada Council for the Arts, and the Province of British Columbia through the British Columbia Arts Council and the Book Publisher's Tax Credit.

Library and Archives Canada Cataloguing in Publication
Title: With/holding / Chantal Gibson.
Other titles: Withholding
Names: Gibson, Chantal N., author.
Description: Poems.
Identifiers: Canadiana 20210198192 | ISBN 9781773860626 (softcover)
Classification: LCC PS8613.I2945 W58 2021 | DDC C811/.6—dc23

with/holding
Poems by Chantal Gibson

Caitlin Press 2021

To us.

Contents

In Lieu of Flowers

HAND WASH COLD WITH
COLORS. DO NOT BLE
DRY IN THE SHADE

LAVAR A MANO CON
CON COLORES SIM
USAR BLANQUEAD
EL TENDEDERO
NO SE DEB

Terms n Conditions

I come to you withholding. Let's
not loiter in the truth. The evil is
already written, our files forever
corrupted. No free antivirus. No

algorithmic way out. The content
is sponsored, baked with our DNA,
the machines busy with the mind-
less work of reproduction. There's

no Science in remembering, no Art
in the daily curation of our suffering,
no wonder in their wretchedness,
no limit to the limits of their artificial

intelligence. That **Error** message—
just a distraction. The evil is set on
a loop. Our horror lies not in what
we consume. It's in the grinning

tyranny of copy n paste, the geno-
ciding rate we feed on our own
afflictions. It's in the dead-ending
ways we spend our pain per diem.

I come to you with holding. These
are the last days of history—swipe
left for Nostalgia—your Compliance
will only result in our Termination.

Let's AGREE the end begins now.
Let *us* Consent to our own *un*doing.

Click Here

Because it is a systemized negation of the other,
a frenzied determination to deny the other any attribute of humanity,
colonialism forces the colonized to constantly ask the question

"Who am I?"

The defensive positions born of this violent confrontation
between the colonized and the colonial constitute a structure
which then reveals the colonized personality.

In order to understand this "sensibility" we need only to study
and appreciate the scope and depth of the wounds inflicted on
the colonized during a single day under a colonial regime.
— *Frantz Fanon*

Holding Patterns

Add To Cart

Product	Description	Price
Favorite Memories iPhone case	Loveable impact-resistant cartoon Golliwog. Comes with striped bowtie and signature red waistcoat. Slim profile. Plastic hard-shell case. Features include blackface, goggle eyes, spikey hair and classic red banana lips.	~~$32~~ $26

Nixxer Baby
onesie

For the Black Americana enthusiast. $29.40

100% cotton. Pre-shrunk. Available in

black and mulatto. 6 to 24 mos.

Ad, Chlorinol.

Bleach.

Machine wash.

Hang dry.

Moorish
bath set   Luxuriously soft brushed

                            microfibre Negress. Comes semi- $44.74

bath mat $21.73
32" x 64"   naked with washtub, necklace, breast
hand towel
15" x 30"   and head scarf.

                            Nude reclining white woman included

                            for extra absorption.

Mammy
throw pillow
14" x 14"

100% polyester poplin maid

adds a statement to any room.

Black and white reproduction

comes with head wrap, neck

kerchief and white apron.

Grin printed on both sides.

Includes concealed zipper

and replaceable insert.

$31.96

Mamie Till-Mobley
canvas print

24" x 24"

Image captured and stretched

on a wooden frame. Delivered

"ready to hang" with mounting

hooks and nails.

$67.74

Justice 4 Breonna
duvet cover

88" x 88"

Luxurious 100% polyester microfibre

bedspread. Fade resistant black and

white print on the front.

Zipper closure on the side.

Queen.

Rest in comfort.

$179.99
$143.99

Frantz Fanon
Cognitive Dissonance
weekender tote

24" x 16"

Perfect for a summer staycation

or a weekend retreat.   Soft spun

poly-poplin fabric. Features durable

double-stitched seams and 1" thick

cotton rope handles for easy carrying

and maximum comfort.

$63.91

Whipped Peter
coffee mug

Fade resistant image.

Comes in black and white.

11oz 15 oz and 20 oz sizes

Microwave safe.

Durable scratch resistant surface.

~~$14.00~~
$ 9.74

I Can't Breathe
face mask

7" x 5"

100% polyester.

Designed for everyday use.

Covers the mouth in public. Ear loops

include adjustable grommets. Fits well on

adult men's faces. Black only.

$26.83

Slave Ship yoga mat	Durable non-slip microfiber surface.	$89.47
24" x 72"	Bottom solid black and punctured	
	for better grip.	
	Image printed across the top. Ships	
	within 1-2 business days.	

whitewash (under lying messages)

During the [insert general time period here] we have taken time to quietly reflect and listen to our valued [customers/associates/fans/friends/employees/stakeholders]. We have made a commitment to change by removing the [name/image/icon] from our [packaging/branding] recognizing it does not reflect our core values. We want to express our solidarity and our deep commitment to taking action. We believe this will make a difference over time. To our loyal [customers/associates/fans/friends/employees/stakeholders] we thank you for your feedback. While the [name/logo/image] has changed we assure you our product will remain the same.

(How to Make) Blackfriends
Sponsored Content

Thinking about naming your country band or start-up after a 19th century historical figure? Or a time period marked by the colonial subjugation and exploitation of Black, Brown and Indigenous people? Well, think again.

If you're planning to use somebody's black face, real or imagined, on your shiny new logo, consult your Black friends right away, before moving ahead with your branding strategy. Just because you remember the taste of penny

candy, or long for your Nana's grinning salt n' pepper shakers, rocking that vintage, old-school vibe ain't what it used to be. A pair of Air Jordans and a grade-seven hip-hop class with cardboard and finger guns won't get you

a Thug Life. The good old days may feel a bit sticky right now, depending on how tight you're holding on to the past. Go ahead, just try to get it off you.

Don't have any "black friends"? Feeling a little dissonance? Take a look around the office, and no, the guy in IT doesn't count. Scroll through your contacts, tap into your network or reach out to HR.

Time for a survey or a focus group? Call a meeting, grab the white board and colored markers. Host a learning lunch, a half-day workshop with half sandwiches, or a weekend revisioning retreat with team t-shirts, ball caps,

yoga mats and tote bags. Perhaps it's time to think about hiring a Black consultant.

If you're an established corporation with a profound appreciation for Black Americana, the time has come to say good-bye to your smiling black friends. You can't work that wholesome Underground Railroad angle forever. Stop

Photoshopping your logo. Swapping the head scarf for a soft perm and pearls won't make her look timeless. Deleting a butler's bow-tie just calls attention to all that PC nonsense. A white-collared Uncle Ben will never look like Barack

Obama, and light Aunt Jemima still looks like Auntie-Blackness. It's hard, letting go. Unless it's fixed to your head, a brown face is still blackface, no matter how you render it. *Say you're sorry. Say they matter. Call it a learning experience.*

Elevate the content. Make a donation. Promote diversity from within—Offer everyone a seat at the table. Try making new BLACK FRIENDS. Find an athlete, an actor, a celebrity scholar, an influencer, a reformed gangster rapper.

It's time for change and authenticity comes at a price.

Don't panic. Spin it.

Call it Reparations.

Call it *Rap!*arations.

Just keep your eye on the bottom line.

Blacklist

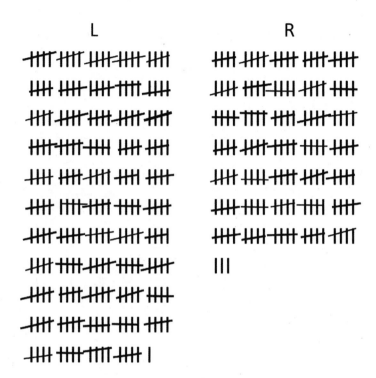

Blackfish

What if I publish a peer-reviewed paper called *Marching Forward,*

Clapping Back: A New Semiotics of Black Womanhood in the Fight

Against White Nostalgia?

Blackfish

What if I cite a study by a scholar, a Black woman who's really

a whte woman wth ssues and a PhD n Afrcan Studes?   What f

* cte her make-up, her perm, her headscarf, and hoops?

Blackfsh

What f she has a whte teenage daughter who gets her beauty tps from an nstagram star an nfluencer wth a blaccent a spray tan and a half a mllon followers?

Bl_ckfsh

Wht f one of them s sttng n the front row
of my classroom? What f * see her n the
sea of whte f_ces?

Bl ckfsh

Wht f *'m cught?

~~Blckfsh~~

Wht f * mgne her || lone?

Wht f * rech out?

Wht f * wrt hr grd schl lttr?

Wht f * gt th sgns ll wrng?

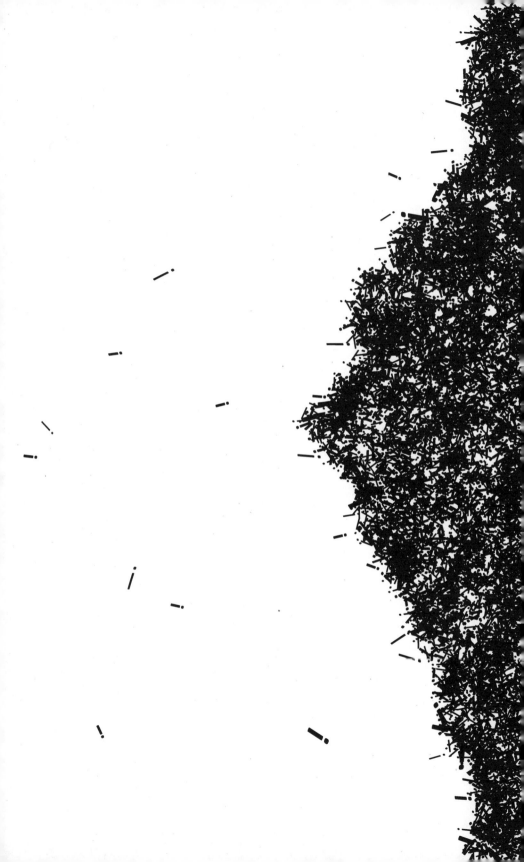

Blackout (Refrain)

i c a n ' t b r e a t h e

i c a n ' t b r e a t h e

i c a n ' t b r e a t h e

i c a n ' t b r e a t h e

i c a n ' t b r e a t h e

i c a n ' t b r e a t h e

i c a n ' t b r e a t h e

i can't breathe

i can't breathe

i can't breathe

ican't breathe

iartbreathe

ërbeate

iade

b

b

b

b

.

on behalf of our ancestors   sent

folded & stacked like black
plastic deck chairs
without return
shipping

to: those who remain   un -   un -

unmoved   un-
              by the bloated head-   un-
lines   by the swollen type-   *un-*
face   by our herniated names   un -

opacified

colour blind

virtue lensed

chalked
with historical
cataracts

who still can't do the math

we leave you

we leave you our eyes

our wide *un-*
blinking eyes

we leave you

our shock
our dismay
our disbelief

we leave you our ears   drumming
                our sonic scars
                our tinnitus

        the shots
        the sirens
        your sonorous shadows

-ing
-ing
-ing

the frequency of our pleas

the frequency of our *PLEASE!*

we leave you our mouths
our swollen sorrow circles

the ~~gaping~~ hole
the howling gouge
the out cry   our snot our spit
                          our cracked lips

we leave you
the grimace
you mistake
for a smile

we leave you our teeth   what's left

of them   our canines   our bit
tongues   our lisping incisors
             our blistered grammar

our busted accents

(now you can use them for free)

we leave you our necks

save your knees
keep the choke-
hold

find new things to do with rope

we leave you our chains
~~all of them~~
metal and metaphor

(but not the gold ones)

we leave you our pain

Rx
TAKE DAILY AS NEEDED TIL FINISHED
NO REFILLS

Watch reruns of our syndicated deaths
between Friends and Law & Order

we leave you our records
   our lists
   our letters
   our literature
   our histories
   our footnotes[1]

1. for when you have to write an essay
(or buy one)

we leave you our records
    our passports
    our passwords
    our emails
                  our feedback
    the HR file
    the EDI survey
    the Human Rights Report

we leave you our records

the vinyl
the tapes

all the shit you haven't stolen

we leave you the N word

      the slights
      the slurs

      the slightly off coloured jokes

go on   say it

put on your #blackface

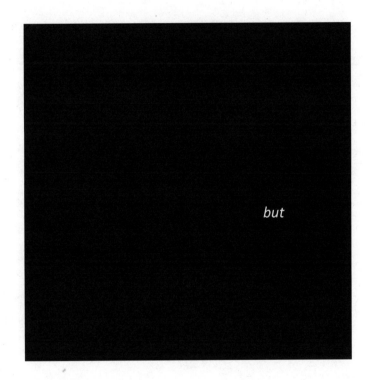

but

we taking our hands

PICK. YOUR. OWN. BEANS.

No sequins
No soles

No soul
No beats

we leave you to clap on

the one

we taking   your friends

           your black friends
           your Black friends
           your "black friends"

the staff, the workers, your supervisor

    the token the pawn
    the diversity hire
    the sister on the cash register
    the brother in the back on the grill

those people up the street

your daughter's playdate
your daughter's girlfriend
your daughter's hookup

your brother's second wife

the maids, the mammies, the magical
negroes   the funny guy that always

dies first

and
we taking   our kids

the glossy one on your brochure

the skinny one on your fridge

from the ~~slave~~ ship to the scholar ship

NO DARK WEB

NO LIVE CAM

NO ~~BREAKING~~ NEWS

no Ivory
no Mars
no Carbon
no Payne's Grey

no shade
no shadows
no silhouettes

no outlines
no borders
no targets

no stars

TAZE *THIS*

ow it feel   wit out us

cold?

wear
a
sweater

white flag

admit me   to this broken thought

hospital   let me step inside and

fill the hollows of that

straight jacket   let me wrap my arms

around my shoulders

and lace it tight   lemmerest inthepull

ofmymadness sitinthehold

ofmyancestors shutthese

eyes quietthisnoise listen

totherhythmofmyDNA

countbackfromoneto23

measure the rise ^{n}fall $_n$

riseofeverybreathhonorthis

bloodandsummonevery

cellthatmadethissorrybody

The insomniac does not have this freedom to sleep, to relax, to doze. The insomniac does not stay awake: it's the night that stays awake.

It stays awake.
　　　　—*Frantz Fanon*

Journal de bord

Phobogenesis

it's the way she bites the heads off first

it's the way she shows her teeth

it's the way she holds up each head

less body like a tiny black trophy be

tween her pinchy-pink finger tips

it's the way she looks right at me and

smiles   my best friend

it's the way she still calls me

   in my sleep

not to be mean   just kidding

it's the way *i* imagine them

inside her   *after* the chewing and

the swallow

theswollenstucktogether

in her belly

it's the Payne's grey lips

it's the anise of anise

it's the way she won't stop talking

it's the sharkish laugh

it's the spit-scum pooling in the corner

of her mouth

it's how she swipes it away

with her shoulder

it's the way she keeps stuffing her hand

in that brown paper bag

                    the hollow

when it's empty

                    the look

on her face

                    when we're gone

Blackwidow

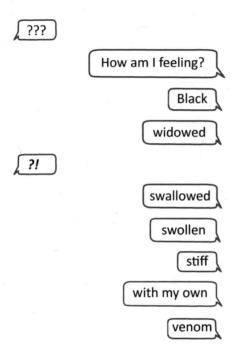

???

How am I feeling?

Black

widowed

?!

swallowed

swollen

stiff

with my own

venom

...

Rotten Tomato

Though not afraid to speak, I did not want to be seen as the one who "spoiled"
the good time, the collective sense of sweet solidarity in blackness.
　　—*bell hooks*

it's how *we* get dressed up to see *Black Panther*
it's the clink of our glasses when we say "to us"
it's the heated debate Chadwick or Michael B.
it's how we sparkle in our custom Black Cougar t-shirts

it's how the theatre's packed to the rafters
it's the apostrophe in Nyong'o
it's the double u in Kaluuya
it's how the Black Diaspora's sittin up front

it's how far we've come to get here
　　Lupita's *Patsey*
　　Michael B's *Oscar Grant*
　　Angela's *Tina Turner*
　　Chadwick's *Jackie Robinson*
　　Forest's *Idi Amin*

it's how i can't suspend my disbelief:

a young Black man, with a Fanonian-
American cousin pock-marked with
kill scars, becomes the leader of the
wealthiest, technologically advanced
country in the world, an African nation un-
touched by colonialism, yet—

404
Page not found

fratricide was the only choice?

it's how i paid to see all this star power
this blockbuster
this Blackbuster
this ★★★★★ dead-ending

no justice
no peace
no catharsis
no sequel

it's how i got my hopes up
it's how Toni Morrison's always right

it's how everyone stays for the credits
it's how *The Women* stole the show

it's how proud *they* look in their t-shirts
it's how we exit single file

it's how one says "don't start" when i ask—
it's how another tells me to *"lighten up"*

Ad Hominem

How we see a thing—even with our eyes—is very much dependent on where
we stand in relationship to it.
      —*Ngũgĩ wa Thiong'o*

in the mornings i walk past your statue
to catch a train across a river with your
name on it, to work at a university that
still bears your name. i have to look up
follow the diagonals of your waistcoat
the open sails of your collar, the winded
kerchief knotted round your ample neck
angular jaw, closed mouth, classic nose
centered, blocky, slightly more than an
eye-length wide, all this to get to your un-
bounded stare, your immortalized gaze.

**TO COMMEMORATE THE DISCOVERY VOYAGE
DOWN THE RIVER BY SIMON FRASER 1808**

on the way to campus, *I* return to my lesson:

- focus on the argument
- avoid personal attacks
- distinguish your ideas from others'
- credit those from whom you borrow
- don't take what's not yours

as I journey down the hallway to my classroom
deeper inside the belly of another ship, my USB
employee ID jangling from the branded lanyard
round my neck, the irony the fucking weight of it is not

lost on me. in the evening, i return home against
the tide. *Stow-low. Stó:lō.* i take the long way not
to look at you. i know it's just a matter of time be-
fore the river takes her name back, the valley and

the canyon too, til we stop saying yours out loud
and kern it to the nub—til we go the way of *KFC*
and our descendants forget what the F stands for.
i know it's just a matter of time before you're de-

faced, beer piss, red paint, *Booster Juice*, til they
wrap a chain around your neck and drag n dump
you in the river. some muddy part of me wants
to gouge *your* eyes out, bitter the sculptor got

them first, while another keeps a watchful eye on
the rising condo markets—and settles for a little

bird shit.

Keynote

some nights i'm at a conference
presenting to an auditorium full
of my peers. there's not enough

room for *us* in the Academy, so
it's always a mad dash for seats,
a lot of side shuffling and sliding

over, unbleached canvas merch
bags holding seats until the name-
tags spill over into the aisles and

down the stairs, until my old high
school principal clears his throat
over the loud speaker and starts

saying "you're breaching the fire
code, those without seats will un-
fortunately have to leave" and so

that's when the room gets all wide-
eyed and *hell-no!* and skinny sisters
start inching over and the big girls

start sucking it *all* in, patting their
thighs like aunties til this plenary
session is stacked three deep, this

neck-rolling-diaspora daring him to
say something now. laughter ripples
over an ocean of programs folded

into church fans. behind the lectern
i'm in heels, hands crossed fig leaf
position, standing atop that *Chlorinol*

soap box. i can't believe i'm up here
being so literal, the two shiny black
babies and the bleached one grinning

out from the logo, *Be like de White*
~~Ninnor~~ partially redacted, up here
inhaling the futile scent of Sharpie.

then the house lights dim. i touch
my hoops, check one-two, tap the
mic and nudge the auditorium with

my black gel nailed fingertip. i take
a deep breath in, roll up on my toes
and lean into the chatter. i say *Good*

Morning and a weighty chorus says
Good Morning! how i cling to this
moment every time, the unison

the generosity, the accents swelling
up this Standard English, sweating
hands, my left thumb hovering over

the clicker, this kinned-kind call n
response, how i'm rocked back
on my heels, *you got this*, swayed

by the heat of a single breath, *we
got you*, held in the darkness, held
by their gaze, til they're slapped

by the whiteness of my first slide,
shock-masked in blue HD screen.
it's too late. *I* can't stop now: the

clicking, the scrolling, the red laser
pointing. I can't stop them from
squinting and adjusting their necks,

the room tilted back disbelieving
the name in bold italics 44-pt font.
Really? Her? they look so pissed,

so betrayed, so disappointed. I ex-
plain, *i-know-i-know, i didn't know,*
i-thought-she-was, this-is-my-worst-

nightmare! and i keep clicking and
pointing to get to the truth, saying
ths sn't real, looklook, t's not what

t looks lke, as the little black **i**'s start
suiciding to the stage as my ancestors
give up in disgrace, as my peers un-

fasten from each other and fill the
exits, as I shout **wat-wat, 'll take a**
DNA test! as my high heels curl into

the splintering soap box, as my high
school principal tells them to walk
single file.

Figure Ground

I'm outside in the hallway, back in the day when
men closed their office doors. I can hear the rise
n fall of a young woman's voice, *White Noise*, spear-

mint, DeLillo this, DeLillo that, Dylar, death, and her un-
dulant giggling. She's nervous, the smart one who
sits up front with the apologetic glasses. I'm eyeing

the 1788 Brookes slave ship diagram, a reproduction
of a reproduction of a reproduction silver thumb-
tacked to my AmLit professor's door. It's always

my first time seeing *them*. Late-starter to university,
late-comer to Black Studies, I'm blank inside, filling up
with the

FIG. I
FIG. II
FIG. III
FIG. IV
FIG. V
FIG. VI
FIG. VII

horror intended by the first abolitionists to ever
post this image in a newspaper or coffee house.
I lean in close, my disbelieving eyes adjusting to

the figure ground. More stupid giggling, some-
thing about simulated reality and distinguishing
words from things. I use the bits of white space

to make sense of the scene, heads, shoulders,
knees n toes, what appears to be hundreds of
black bodies, women, men, girls, boys aligned

in rows, the twice fucked-over curved round
the masts and bow, each posed, hands folded
over privates in the fig leaf position. I begin

counting with my right pointy finger **FIG. V**
Section H top row, first closest to the stern,
that's when one of them drops to the floor and

the hallway floods with anise. At first it looks 2D
flat like a shadow, like a hole in the beige carpet,
and then it breathes and two tiny arms come un-

stuck, like a gooey Rorschach, two tiny fists reach
up as if to say, *m'fucker, pick me up!* and so i pick
it up and put it in my coat pocket, then i see the

gap I've left behind, so i touch the figure next to
the white space and that one falls too. i tap the
next and the next and the next and the next un-

til a black-beckoning cluster forms on the floor
and the air is black licorice. i pull my shirt collar
up over my nose and return to the map now un-

dulating with elbows and the shuffling of legs
towards the exit, like *we'bout to get the fuck
outta here!* so i spread my coat on the floor for

the jumpers, careful to block the bottom of the
door, the way you do in case of fire to keep the
smoke from wafting into the office. i hear chairs

shuffling, almost over, she's stopped talking shit
about Hitler and Elvis and the rise of the novelty
intellectual. i can hear the chipped pink polish on

"   "

her finger quotes and oh my fucking god that laugh
and time is running out and i am only on **FIG. IV
Section G** trying to get the women and children

out first. The door knob is turning and there goes
the latch, so i release my collar both hands flailing
tap-tap-jabbing fingers unfolding them free falling

to the floor, but I'm still too slow, sticky, gooey on
fumes, their tiny arms crossed, heads shaking, they
know I'm a late-starter, a late-comer, a constant dis-

appointment, and when the professor opens the
door and looks down at me on all fours, all guck-
mouth and black teeth, he says, "Wait your turn,

I'll be with you in a minute."

Old Souls, Halifax 1950

...it was not always a single event that was the cause of the symptom, most often on the contrary, it arose out of multiple traumas, frequently analogous and repeated...
    —*Frantz Fanon*

she's born   pissed
every time

my mother   sideways   star-
stretched   elbows n   knees

a rebel   protest baby   fighting *not*
to come out

       *One life-time with white folks was quite
       enough—thank you very much!*

she folds   like
a fist   afightingknot

refuses to cry   *no*
matter   how

many times
i slap her

still-born-bitter
a century after

a sentry   after *this* dis/
enchanted womb

    she takes it all in vitro the news
    the shitty water   the smell
    of garbage   the segregated
    whispers n suck teeth   the hour-

long walk up Barrington the un-
paved roads   hard right at
Cornwallis   old-timey servants'
entrance   around-back

the sagging middle step
the sinewy creak
in her mother's knees

the affectation of white-
aproned *Good Morning*s

the percussing grammar
of the modern breakfast
table come to life:

clink of tiny juice glasses
the matte-rattle of plastic forks
the mint-green rhythm of melamine plates

the bump
of hungry white children

instant coffee
instant cereal
instant grinning pancake mix

add eggs
add water
add milk

THIS is progress

at night *i* follow them *back to Africville*
this-mother-my-mother-inside-her

at night she floats

                                                            cell-kin

in the amniotic hold

                                        single

of our ancestors   they wait for her   every

our entire blood   lined up

                    wave of   a chorus

                              arms
to the horizon: an   un folding

                              stretched

            out
                              of elbows

                                                        to her

                                                back
with holding
            the journey   of hands past   passed-passing all the way

                                    back

                        to her

first mother

a squint   of blood   of pulse   of drums   of iris   of cheek

bones rising   of lips   of teeth   of breath   of herb   of animal   of

language   squint of fire   squint of sun

rise   squint of morning   of freedom   of wind   of ocean   squint

of ocean   squint of salt   of salt

of   of salt

ocean

                                              of salt

of

                                                   of

of once

of free

of Black

of Loyalist

of black wench

a black wench

a one-way ticket from Halifax to   Sierra Leone

with no   intention   of coming

back

she protests
when the pushing starts
fist over fist she's half-way up the um-

bilical chord before the suck n
pull

of the new baby-
turning-grabbing machinery   she curls

into a tiny hug
until her lungs
s u r r e n d e r

to the air—
she takes it all in

white lights
ammonia

disappointed
every time
i hold her

betrayed
every time
i whisper

*"Don't worry   it's me
you'll be alright   this time"*

before *they*
hand me the scissors

before *i*
make the fatal cut

Other Ways of Knowing, Expo 67

i am the daughter of a tight-lipped
woman whose people go all the way
back to Aunt ███s house, an out of

wedlock baby, a fifth half-sibling
a one-time father from Trinidad or
Barbados or St. Kitts, the other one

the dark one, the one who looks like
sin and smells like bleach, first one
to the table, last one to eat, the one

in the corner scraping burnt rice from
the pot with the dull edge of a kitchen
knife til my mother's nerves split and

her back teeth come loose. That's why
i know to soak the pan in warm soapy
water while i sweep the kitchen floor.

By kindergarten, i'm facilitating work
shops, PowerPoint, *Zoom*, breakout
rooms, *How to Clean a White Lady's*

House. Born hip to this handmedown
life, i find small comfort in the quiet
folding of clothes. i'm a know-it-all

a big mouth, a deep gouge from Guys-
borough to Halifax. At 16, i meet my
daughter's father down at the docks

a Polaroid sailor, an apprentice crew-
man, a sepiatoquedhipster from just out-
side Montreal. We make a mockery

of my knee socks and desecrate the
belly of the *Bluenose II*. In the men's
quarters i conceive a way out of this

mess, scratch the wooden ceiling of
his berth with my kilt pin, one hatch
mark for every day i follow him up the

St. Lawrence til we dock at Cité du
Harve. i give birth right there inside
Arthur Erickson's *Man and Community*

Pavilion, capsized by a violent brush
with the future, the spire, a slender
pyramid of trellis, my climbing gaze

tiny circle of light, the smell of West
Coast forest, dark mirrored hallway
and a room of plaster statues, face-

less white figures in cages, locked
in the hollows of anomie. Clearly in-
visible, never meant to be here, i go

right and leave them to their white-
people problems, not ready for Papa
Ibra Tall, Senegalese painter *here!?*

how epic the black man throwing off
the choke of colonialism, modernist
brush stroke, his mutinous colour

palette, his telepathic Africans, not
ready for this gut-punch of optimism
a kick in my belly and the gush of

water down my thighs. After Expo 67
i pack up my kid and buy a one-way
train ticket, flip my black middle-

finger at her entire paternal line who
(quietly) prefer the company of white
folk. In Toronto, i show'em all a little

Négritude, say "She's *Black*" out loud
if anyone raises an eyebrow. i'm cold
winter jacket from September to June

til someone calls me Jamaican. i get
some social assistance, go to secretary
school, get my short-hand, a Legal Aid

job, and a two-bedroom apartment
with my girlfriend, a white woman
with 2 kids and 1 good eye. At night

we stay up late and enjoy a little *Tia
Maria* with our cribbage. That's why
my kid's so good at counting—15

two 15 four 15 six and a pair is eight
—and tallying scores. On weekdays,
i am all Angela Davis, straight up!

Black Panther behind my steno note
pad, pink line down the middle, bull-
shit on the left, Truth on the right.

i take it all down, all of it—the stories
of brown folks with shitty white people
problems, what the witness said, what

the cops said, the social worker, the
lawyers, the judge, what happened and
what really happened between the

silences

known history of fists and swollen
lips, broken tongues and busted
accents, dislocations, relocations

violations and assaults, the usual
holding patterns of injustice. i can
tell who's lying and who's telling

the truth—it's in the quick well of
the eyes. Some days the gravity's just
too much. When i get that knotted

fist in my throat, i don't turn away,
i turn inward, take a step back into
that quiet space behind my eyes

the dark room with the empty chair
and the sign that says **For Humans Only**
i take a seat, take a slow, deep breath

and hold

          L   **R**

and guess which side the first tear

will drop. On weekends, i find some
catharsis in other forms of sanctioned
violence. i watch my black n white TV

like church. Friday nights, i worship
at the altar of Gwen 'Skinny Minnie'
Miller, 5-foot nothing, a monument

no bigger than a minute, rollin up
like a ghost to slap, punch n kick a
white girl with impunity. It's fake,

roller derby, but there's something
about this crowd loving this Black
woman, believing she's Canadian

every time she launches her body
like a missile to break up the pack
or put Sweet Stephanie on her ass.

On Sundays, it's Sweet Daddy Siki
preaching from the center of the
wrestling ring. Black skin, bleach

blond afro, striped shorts, glitter
cape and those *boots!* The future
in colour, in black n white. *Maple*

Leaf Gardens goes crazy when he
steps through the ropes, this Black
Adonis, circle, clench, break, circle,

clench break, kick punch, hold—

history repeating itself, that white
arm round Siki's neck, the show of
force, the test of wills, the slow un-

folding, the wink, the grin, the es-
cape, the shuffle and flying drop-
kick, Black body white boots to the

chest, Black body white boots to
the chest, Black body white boot
to the chest—and the pin

one, two and

Error
Oops! Something went wrong.
Please try again later.

Trolling Cape Coast Castle

i've memorized the tour guide's script, mapped
the route start to finish. now i follow the tourists
slip in behind them when no one's watching and
assume the spot behind someone else's camera
just to see where the lens will take me. no roots-
seeker, no homecomer, no culturalanthropologist
i embed myself amongst the descendants of slaves
and slave traders, a jaded spirit, and watch them
take it all in, the narrative, a brief history of fluids
pissshitvomitmenstrualbloodbeatingsrapesandun-
wanted pregnancies, the death, dying, letting go.
i watch them aim their phones in the dark when
the guide raises his hand to mark the exact height
of human excrement and wait for a flicker, a tiny
seizure before the burst, the algorithm wondering *what
the fuck's worth seeing here* before it fills the dungeon
with automaticflash. most nights i just scrub thru
the holding cells, cross the cobblestone courtyard
by the sea and pass through **TheDoorofNoReturn**
the museum, the coffle, the hold, the slaveshipdia-
gram, the auctionblock and WhippedPeter, just to
get to the giftshop. sometimes i follow celebrities
to see who mourns best. i leave behind two crying
emojis, a row of black fists, and a comment rating
our Ghanaian guide on his knowledge, delivery
and good english.

tonight the camera bypassed the church, my tour
ended in 2017 in a yellow room with peeling walls
and white plinths, atop each one a cement head,
Nsodie, a young Ghanaian artist drawing on the
Akan tradition of creating portraits of the dead
ancestors drawn from the memory of the Black
Diaspora, noses, lips and eyes in varying states of
swollen, each one fashioned, more or less with
a neck:

one looks confused
one looks parched
one looks remorseful

one looks shocked
one looks ashy
one looks a little short sighted

one looks left
one looks right
one looks a bit shifty

one looks up
one looks down
one looks undecided

one looks pale
one's out of breath
one's got a migraine

one's epileptic
one's catatonic
one's in cardiac arrest

one's been duped
one deserves an apology
one thinks there's been a misunderstanding

one's lost sight
one's lost sight of a child
one's looking for the nearest exit

one thinks mama's still in back
one thinks she may be just up head
one's like *this* is some bullshit

pissed betrayed disappointed

lookin at me like *Girl please! Go
to sleep. You don't have better ways
to spend your time?*

Anchors

There was a time when everything we needed to know
was already written and printed and loaded on a truck
by 5am. 5Ws. 1H. That's it. The entire *world* came flat
n folded, 1 colour image on the front. Local, national, inter-

national, everything slid under a welcome mat. Back
then I could roll it up, tuck it under my arm, pop it in
a mailbox, toss it on a lawn or a driveway. Next day,
I could just throw it away, or line the kitty litter box.

My grandfather's TV news took 15 minutes. After dinner,
three-letter-network-men in white shirts and dark neck
ties told serious stories in black and white about kings
and queens, prime ministers and presidents. They called

it reporting, what happened when the people followed
their rulers. They marked the daily measurements, fixed
the world view on a map, and set straight the social order.
They called it breaking news, when sometimes trouble-

makers stepped out of line, like those Birmingham kids
that skipped school and took to the streets marching for
their civil rights. In Halifax, my 13-year-old mother watched
those white police officers load colored children into buses

and cart them off to jail. Out the window there was singing
and two girls smiled for the camera. One had two braided
plaits, the other a fresh finger wave, like they'd dressed up
for jail, like protesting was fun. Her father said, *Girl don't go*

getting any of your bright ideas. The next day, the police
came back with fires hoses and German Shepherds. After
the cardigan sweater attack, her mind added dogs to her
fear list, not German Shepherds, dogs, all dogs holding the

#2 spot between the deadly Black Widow spider she'd seen once in a 4th grade encyclopedia and white people. It was all happening in black n white in America, broadcasting in her living room, small screen flickering behind her eyelids. Back

then, you *watched* the news. You sat still and paid attention. It was all moving so fast. You couldn't move, you couldn't look away for fear of missing out. No repeats. No do-overs. Some- times, the three-letter-men returned at night with an update, a **Bullet-**

-in, to stop the world so everyone could get some sleep.

That's why they called them *anchors.*

Now the news is always breaking, always watching, pinging my pockets, hungry for Blackfolkswhitecops, hourly bullet- ins, weighted with hashtags and Getty images, my grand- father's news reincarnated on my tiny screen, same head-

lines, same stories, same songs, same nightsticks, same #Fear Of Missing Out—this is not nostalgia. At night, i watch those three-letter-men on YouTube, think about how we took it all in, shitty graphics, crappy sound, static, blur, how fogged the

lens, how we believed we were seeing everything so clearly, how quickly we convinced ourselves we were watching the truth.

Forensic Report
December 28, 2020 - April 28, 2021

1.

It's about the way *The New York
Times* laid out her home for the re-
creation. It's about nearly 1,000,000

YouTube views. It's about the over
10,000 comments and the nearly 3.5
million subscribers, and the fact that

i'm one. It's about going over all of
the evidence, the reports, recordings
and crime scene photos, the lemon

yellow sauce pan, the small blue one
hiding inside, the pot holders and the
oven mitts hooked on the wall above

the sink, and the folded dish cloth
draped over the tap. It's about the
burgundy throw pillows against

the sage green sofa and the gap be-
tween the seat cushions, like some
body just got up. It's about that

Yoki rainbow sequined sneaker and
a purple blouse and Exhibit 47, the
beige bra with the tag sticking out:

HAND WASH COLD WITH
DO NOT BLEACH
DRY IN THE SHADE

LAVAR A MANO CON
CON COLORES SIM
USAR BLANQUEAD
EL TENDEDERO
NO SE DEB

It's about all the clicking, pausing and
zooming in, trying to get at the truth.
It's about my sweaty hands, my swollen

hashtags, and my scrolling heartrate.

Article continues below

2.

It's about mapping an accurate time-
line of events. It's about precision and
erasure, a grey-scale diagram, a linear

floorplan and my bird's eye view of her
home. It's me calling out, my choking
silence, a futile god tapping my screen

to nudge her awake. It's how I know
it's another bad dream, seven white
cops lined up, guns drawn, outside her

door. It's not real. It's an animation
like a scene from a videogame, like *Call
of Duty* or *Counter-Strike,* the shit my

students play, it's just they're all white,
the cops, not white-people-white, hyper
white, screen white

like cotton
like titanium
like powdered sugar
like detergent
like cocaine
like...

moonlight

white hands, white weapons, same white
body shape, same white featureless face,
same empty expression. Marked only by

black body armor and the word POLICE,
they're blanks, like white plastic army
figures, like rigged 3D avatars with-

out their skins. It's how the two of them
look flat in bed, like shadows, like targets,
like gendered restroom signs, like IKEA.

3.

It's about how every room in this spacious
two-bedroom apartment comes fitted with
standard features. Basic furniture and

large appliances, fridge, stove, sofas, chairs,
tables, beds, lines, circles, rectangles, squares,
san serif font, everything comes in white.

BEDROOM
BATHROOM
HALLWAY
KITCHEN
LIVING AREA

Accessories not included.

Where's the *HOME* sign on her front door?

Her blue Louisville EMT jacket on the back?

The three canvas prints set on the diagonal?

Good Times

Good Wine

Good Friends

What about the tousle of black n white duvet?

And the persistent clothes hamper next to the bed?

Article continues below

Get your whites whiter.

4.

It's about the neighbor's
black and white door mat:

**NOTHING INSIDE IS
WORTH DYING FOR**.

5.

Interview Room 2:
Camera 2   2020-03-13

It's about 04:04 am

It's about how he says she
"popped up out of sleep"
when she heard the *BANG!*
at the front door

It's about three hours after
the dog and driveway sirens

It's about another brother in
a white room under oath

this time a camera and a blue-
lined note-pad, 2 more white
cops, a table, a tape recorder

It's about the bottom of that
tissue box, his voice inflamed
and swollen from pleading

how it cracks a bit, when he says

"It scared her to death. Me, too."

      Given the spectrum of death,
      that statement was not entirely
      untrue. An idiom uttered in an

      affidavit, under the humming
      life-suck of florescent light,
      may hold a flicker of truth.

      It's something, really, how we
      learn to not say what we really
      mean, and yet, mean everything

we say, how we mash words into
sticky signifiers and feed them to
our young, how we binge them on

a steady diet of metaphor, save
room for hyperbole, how we be-
lieve what we want then swipe

away the excess at the corners,
like when my cousin writes *Omg,*
I'm dying! when she gets a ❤

by an Instagram star. The truth is
in there somewhere, it's a moving
target, you just have read the signs—

It's about an act of faith at this
point, the cops listening to him

centuries of programming, finding
the evidence, what it was exactly

that died inside of him that night,
recording the ebb of his breath

and the flow of tears, the snot,
the phlegm, the empty box and

the crushed bouquet of beige-
fisted tissues—the *first* memorial

right there in front of them.

6.

What about that red cellphone case
on the ground outside right next
to the *Welcome* mat?

7.

And what about the evidence?

What about the hatch

marks and right-angled rulers on her
windows framing the bullet holes? Black lines in rows

against a white background. Centimeters. Millimeters.
What exactly is the unit of measure? Are we counting

the black marks or adding the whiteness between them?

A bullet hole is represented with a 2D circle, erasing the
cracked corona shatter round it. A round is never round.

Here lies the myth of forensic precision. It's about how
Science, like History, rounds off

those jagged edges.

Revisionist History
May 3, 1963 — June 7, 2017

leave it to a nerdy, light-skinned brother
from Ontario, with an afro and a stupid IQ
to start asking questions. give him a pod-
cast and watch him knock the soap box out
from under your feet: turns out the 1963
Birmingham cardigan sweater attack cap-
tured on the front page of *The New York
Times*, didn't happen the way my mother
remembered it. turns out the Foot Soldier
monument in Kelly Ingram Park—around
the corner from the memorial dedicated
to the four Black girls murdered in the 16th
Street Baptist Church bombing—
isn't entirely true

THIS SCULPTURE IS DEDICATED TO THE FOOT SOLDIERS
OF THE BIRMINGHAM CIVIL RIGHTS MOVEMENT.
WITH GALLANTRY, COURAGE AND GREAT BRAVERY
THEY FACED THE VIOLENCE OF ATTACK DOGS,
HIGH POWERED WATER HOSES AND BOMBINGS.

turns out the tall skinny cardigan brother
was just an onlooker caught in the chaos

turns out the white cop was pulling up
on the leash holding the dog back

turns out the sculptor had his own
interpretation of the events

turns out the mayor of Birmingham told
part of the story

turns out Black History Month is *cancelled*

turns out black widows aren't that deadly

turns out I could have had a dog after all

Fanon's Couch

And in one sense, if I had to define myself I would say I am in expectation; I am investigating my surroundings; I am interpreting everything on the basis of my findings. I have become a sensor.
　　—*Frantz Fanon*

i.

it's been over 20 years since grad school, since
Amadou Diallo, since the beginning of the end
of hardcover books, since the piercing dawn of
dial-up, since *I* read you in post-colonial studies

my renowned professor, her curated reading list,
Bhabha, Kristeva, Spivak, always already epistem-
ologically speaking, our ontologically rectangular round-
table, her pointed questions, *why are you here?*
no-wait-wait *what are you doing here?*

~~here~~, her …

my disappointing silence

　　　　　　　　　　　　　　　　I guess

i'm her in *A Map to the Door of No Return* the cliché
making my "way grudgingly and insecurely through
academia, through life, never sure, always sure she
is never in control"

　　　　　　so i'm her here now trying to make
some sense of this mess. Nearly 35 years after Ngũgĩ
Colonialism　and Capitalism　and COPS　still remain
the C words of the day　　we're *still* discussing what
it means to decolonise

i attended a CanLit conference
a few years ago, sat in a small circle on a hard-plastic
folding chair in the 'allyship tent' pitched out-side the
main venue, while inside, a white man, a self-defined
immigrant, stands up and says, *I came here 30 years
ago, I love it. I don't get it, why are the brown people
here so angry?*

*"That's great, Sir. Good for you. But it's important not
to essentialize your experience."*

my body knows this answer, tattooed on my brain 20
years ago as i suddenly relive the night my friend James
took me to see Dr. Angela Davis at the *Vogue Theatre* in
Vancouver. there was an elder, a song and drumming,
my first land acknowledgement. then Dr. Angela Davis,
the first *Black Panther,* lectured on the incarceration of
Black, Brown and Indigenous women in Australia and
the United States. last in the queue of dreadlocks and
shaved heads, behind a line of green khaki social justice
freaks, a white man, a European immigrant takes the
mic: *I've lived here 30 years, I love it here. I don't get it,
why are you so angry?*

now i've got a classroom
and a book deal and i'm out in the world doing lectures
talking about decolonising my mind, like it's just the be-
ginning, like it's new information, like it's still possible,
like there's hope, meanwhile, i'm stuck at home scrolling
the body count as Black and Brown folk, men-women-girls-
boys get fucked over on the daily, like i'm not so sure any
more

add Covid and Corona

we're all wearing masks, we're still
wearing masks, like so many
fucking masks

ii.

i bought new copies of *Black Skin White Masks* and
The Wretched of the Earth and *The Psychiatric Readings*,
published in Canada and the United States of America,

paperbacks. i'm trying to respect your rights, trying not
to *participate in or encourage electronic piracy of copy-
righted material,* just like your publisher asked me to.

Electronic Piracy—that's <u>a thing</u>. it's a shit-show really,
what's happened to information since your first edition.
Please consider me *a reviewer*, before i start marking up

these pages with yellow highlighter and sticky notes.

iii.

like you, "I am not the bearer of absolute truths."
i want you to know i read to the end. i *know* i know
there are Yes days, Yes to life, Yes to love, Yes to
generosity, but today is *not* a Yes day

it's a No-day
   a No-more-day
   a No-nonsense-day

   a No-*no*-*no!*-not-again-day

 a *No-fucking-way!*-day

iv.

some days i think of you, like you just pop into my head

like the day i was invited to a video game design critique,
the day i asked a group of students why their characters
were all white, the day i let the air out of a classroom

like the day i tried to make my own 3D avatar, followed
the YouTube software tutorial step by step and learned
how to apply a brown skin over a standard white mesh

like today i read the front page of the *Globe and Mail*,
"not enough light," young Black Concordia Student
prompted twice by a computer algorithm, a facial recog-

nition system programmed by a human being, to light her
face with a lamp to take an online exam. some days i think
of you, what it would be like now if you'd lived, the head-

lines if you'd survived, you'd be ninety-five, a total
ancestor

like, what if you came back...?

v.

like you, i don't know who first "complained that he had
arrived too late and everything had already been said,"

but the Nostalgia you spoke about is still a thing, but
it's not about remembering the good old days, it's all

about manufacturing them. i know nothing of Aeschylus
but you can order his bust online on a tote bag, a ball

cap, or a 100% cotton t-shirt. now, they call it vintage
or retro, and the 1980s are ancient. even your *Y a bon*

Banania has an afterlife. under threat of "offending
human dignity," the Company let go of the 80-year old

copyright in 2006, yet the grinning goes on, posters,
clocks, towels, greeting cards and mini-skirts, TAGGED

with the same *Uncle Remus minstrel-cannibal-savage
bullshit* you railed about. funny how things just *keep*

coming full circle. vicious isn't it? Europe's mad algo-
rithm for sick African shit—same code, same files

still uploading…

in 2020. get ready for the future. today's technology's
got no moral compass. Colonialism is Globalization's

bitch.

if you're coming back, you'd better step up your game.

vi.

for the record, you will never see me eat
a banana in public. something about dicks.
and still way too much monkey stuff.

vii.

remember when you were on the train, the em—
pty seats next to you? remember being aware of
your body, your own objectifying gaze, not just ex-
isting in the third person, but in triple, your body,
your race, your ancestors?

i'm seeing everything in threes these days. i know
i'm not responsible for my race or my ancestors,
but some part of me is dying, a slow Black death
i'm widowing from the Diaspora spirit-punctured
bit by bit from the daily bulletins, more shrapnel
than descendent, my coffled data, linked and lined-
up on ships, naked, kneeling, lynched and hanging
from trees, archival images, stolen, digitized and up-
loaded to some DIY merch site by some nostalgic
Black Americana enthusiast

                              when African-American
artist Willie Cole reimagined the iconic image of a
18th century slave ship on an ironing board in 1997,
he invoked his Mama, his Aunties and his Ancestors,
the Trinity. who knew some white Cape Town hipster
couple with a bent view of art history and a case of
parasitic activism would repurpose the image on a
line of products for domestics? and who knew how
many of America's Finest would appropriate the fuck
out of British Museum catalogues to hock everything
from cell phone cases to yoga mats?

i can't stop seeing Whipped Peter, the brother with
with the tally marks on his back otherwise known as
Gordon. Google Civil War, Civil Rights, no matter, it's
the only photographic image of its kind. he's trapped
in the public domain. you can download his 1863 carte
de visite from his Wikipedia page, one century before
Birmingham, watch just about any Black History Month
documentary, find him on a wall at Cape Coast Castle
or on a ceramic coffee cup commemorating the ~~end~~
~~of the~~ American Civil War for ~~14.99~~ $9.95.

                          remember when you said,
"an individual who loves Blacks is as 'sick' as some-
one who abhors them?" i admit to some late-night trolling
and there's always someone buried in the comments

calling out **What-the-fuck-is-wrong-with-you?!**
shocked, like I used to be, by the willful disregard for
Black Life and for Black Souls continuing the snatch n
grab tradition of economic exploitation and cultural
appropriation, justifying their actions with some

This-is-a painful-part-of-our-history bullshit

followed by a coward's chorus of **We-must-*never***

-forget-the-past!

Who's this *we* m****r f****r?!

viii.

it's this grinning sentimentality, this bullshit
abolition
                    this gaslighting nostalgia machine

this neck wringing remembering:

it's the GOLLYWOG page on <u>Pinterest</u> *today*

it's the banner message across the top:

> **"People have reported Pins from this search.**
> **Let us know if you see anything against our policies."**

it's the video ad on replay sponsored by OREO

it's the dark cookie dipped in white milk, dipped
in white milk dipped in white milk dipped in white
milk dipped in white milk dipped in white milk dipped in white
milk dipped in white milk dipped in white milk dipped in white
milk dipped in white milk dipped in white milk dipped in white
milk dipped in white milk dipped in white milk dipped in white
milk dipped in white milk dipped in white milk dipped in white
milk dipped in white milk dipped in white milk dipped in white

it's the *Perfect Pairing*

ix.

i see the masks so clearly now: **howimstuck**

in the purgatory of somebody's not giving a f***

the signifier

how far

from

the signified

i guess *that's* why

why I'm always so angry why I'm always so angry why I'm always so angry why I'm always so angry why I'm always so angry

x.

yes, there are better days, small signs of progress, like when a friend from the allyship tent emails you a link to a **BBC News article in 2019** and you learn that works by Monet, Matisse, Picasso and other French masters have been temporarily renamed by the curators of a show in Paris, for the Black female models who sat for them. The *Portrait of a Negress* by Marie-Guillemine Benoist was renamed *Portrait of Madeleine*. Madeleine. the BBC News website respectfully cropped the Getty image above the bare breast, but you can buy the uncut version online for $26.01 US + shipping.

now, i don't mean to get all bell hooks and ruin the good times, i know-i know i'm reading too much into this, but i just don't get it—why is their first thought to change the name? if you really give a shit about this sister, cancel the show and drape a cardigan over her shoulders.

xi.

remember when you said, "there are too many

idiots on this earth?" i wish i could hear you say

that out loud, i wish i could hear your voice just

once, so i can *Pin it* in my head, cadence, timbre

accent, the tiny spaces between words, the rise

n fall of your breath. you're all over

YouTube—same photo, striped tie, a thousand

backgrounds, conference papers, expert inter-

views, public lectures, student projects and study

notes: somewhere a teacher believes Africa is a

country, that our ancestors were passengers on

great big ships. somewhere primary

school children are twisted

on their bellies
handstofeet
inboatpose
doing slavery

yoga.

it's laughable, a mad algorithm, but

not even you could have imagined this

kind of violence...

xii.

in the end, you spoke of monuments

a white man and a black man hand in hand

you too had hope   once

now   i see the end   of monuments

the ~~empty~~ spaces
the busted pedestals
the broken swastikas
the bitter flowers
the hard feelings
their heroes
their martyrs
their ghosts

        my belly kerns
        with the thought
        that our liberation
        is in their hands

xiii.

i didn't see your masks back then
i'm sure my Professor mentioned

them, your education, your white
coat, your lens, Adler, Lacan, Hegel,

Freud, Jung, Sartre and, of course,
your beloved Césaire. You were

a man of your time.

xiv.

you said you married a European
you didn't say a white woman
i wish i could hear you speak

i know it's not all black n white

like you, sometimes i'm with-

holding

xv.

if you do come back, you will have some un-
learning to do. about *us*. times have changed.

Anna Freud didn't consider Black women
women in her research. given time, i think

you'd take back page 134 and drop—
all that Oedipal shit

xvi.

i see masks   everywhere

i think i'm seeing   them

so clearly

and yet

i miss   the obvious

like when you talk   to me

in English
                    and *i* forget

I'm reading   you

in translation

I found a place of sanctuary in "theorizing," in making sense out of what was happening. I found a place where I could imagine possible futures, a place where life could be lived differently...

When our lived experience of theorizing is fundamentally linked to processes of self-recovery, of collective liberation, no gap exists between theory and practice.
    —bell hooks

In Lieu of Flowers

unmasking Nostalgia

where are you from?

the Greek
nóstos meaning *homecoming*
álgos   meaning *pain* or *ache*—

not your name

my origins? I was coined by a Swiss
doctor in his 1688 dissertation—

No, where are you really *from?*

really from?

Yes, before *language*

I'm the melancholy expressed
by a group of Swiss mercenaries
fighting in Italy and France

your <u>Wiki</u> says you're a disorder, a medical condition...

a homesickness
a pining for native pastures
and mountain landscapes

symptoms?

fainting, fever, indigestion
upset stomach, diarrhea

cause?

hypothesis: brain and ear damage
the constant clang-*ing* of cowbells

cowbells?

cowbells.

*so ALL THIS started with a group
of white European men paid to
fight in foreign armies 300-400
miles away from home?*

later, I was loaned to the English
in the 1700s for the melancholy
of colonial seamen longing to
return home

*the 1700s... so what is the word
for 12.5 million longings?*

I beg your pardon?

the term for the condition of my ancestors?

I'm sorry, I don't—

*i mean, what language captures
the melancholy of their captivity,
a five-century migraine, the dis-
order of 6000 miles?*

Now, you're taking me out of
context. These days *I'm* more
a yearning, a wistfulness, a looking ba—

What do you mean, I'm *more?*

What do you mean—

What does the I'm *stand for?*

I'm I'm sorry, you're just
not making any sense.

Greek, Swiss, English, you're
essentially—a white man's problem

Oh, that sounds racist.

racist?

Well, I have been applied more broadly
across different cultures

like Imperialism?

Now, you're purposefully missing
the point—

so, do Black and brown folks experience Nostalgia?

Hello! I'm universal!—anyone with a past, a memory
worth holding on to

what if one person's nostalgia is
another's nightmare? whose counts?

Whoever's make sense

Whoever's make cents

???

you're an abstraction

an ache

a distraction

an aching signifier in search of
its signified

that's bullshit

I'm wanting

exploitive

reclaimed

you're a sellout

an influencer

a long way from cowbells

Yes, indeed
   —with no looking back!

State Sanctioned Violence

When asked if he thought the photograph was racist, he said,
"Yes it was. I didn't consider it racist at the time, but now we
know better."
       —*TIME, September 18, 2019.*

it's *not* the photograph—

it's the lens it's 2001 the new millennium
the future a private school gala   *Arabian
Nights* a fairytale fundraiser   a few bucks short
on imagination

it's the subject a 29-year-old man a white
man a high school teacher   son of a Prime
Minister a workplace function a turban and
blackface clearly a white man without Black
friends

it's the composition   the face neck and hands
the careful attention to coverage right hand over
her shoulder just so sure of itself like a West Van
lady's artisanal necklace creeping over the breast
bone   grinning white teeth   left hand hovering
at *her* waist

it's the setting all the gathering around the chit
chat and speeches   all the posing just out-
side the frame   a night of withholding   a telltale
sign no one asked   *Don't you think that's racist?*

No one whispered, *Dude, look around, there's brown folks here, wash that shit off
or go the fuck home!*

it's not the photograph   it's the white balance

it's *not* the blackface   it's *all* the white masks

underneath

The Punctum Suite: How to Bear Witness, Notes from Mamie Till-Mobley

I. on reading images

punc•tum:

Look at the mask.

[1] *a distinct point*

Look at my boy.

Stare at the   in between.

II. on visual literacy

—Not the first Black casket mother

this time there would be evidence, a life

TIME captured in distress, held for-

ever in this dress, a modest print for

the afterlife, tiny figures, black and

white, two-legged, some four, human-

animal-bird-horse playful, naïve—innocent

reminiscent of a young child's un-

studied hand—and yet   significant

signifying, monumental, calling forth

the rock drawings of the ancients, no not

Lascaux, not Chauvet, not Chapter 1 of

Europe—but Yes! to the Preface of Africa

hatch marked back 100,000 years when

our first Ancestors, *our* first Ancestors

chose to record that which was important

to make visible our lives

our love our loss

our humanity.

2. *a detail in a photograph unintended by the photographer that triggers a thought or visceral reaction that propels the viewer beyond the fact of the image*

III. care instructions

It gives me a chance to get out what is clogged up inside,
because if I don't talk, it stays in and worries me... If I can
let it go, even though I cry sometimes, I have some relief.
     —*Mamie Till-Mobley*

hold

before you blink

[3.] *tiny valves in the upper and lower eyelids near the nose that pump and release tears*

mind the ache in your throat

honor the knotted fist wedged be

tween your vocal chords

flare of nostril

quiver of lip

tiny pump

welling

weight

of salt

then let it go

i's
close
your eyes
honor the first
the path it makes
for the rest

#unfollow

(for Breonna)

i watch you touch your fading pulse
i watch you leave your shadow on the floor
i watch you leave your coat behind
and drop your phone case at the door

i watch you pace the WAITING ROOM, ready
for the ambulance, and when the EMERGENCY
doors slide open, when they wheel the gurney
through the ENTRANCE, you take hold of the cart
and say, I got this.

i follow you down the hallway past the TRAUMA unit

til you're a black silhouette
til your tiny-self looks back
til your raised hand says that's enough
til you turn right at the horizon

EMT (Emancipation Modification Therapy)

It was the first viral image of the brutality of slavery that the world saw...
Which is interesting, when you put it into perspective with today and social
media and what the world is seeing, again. You can't fix the past, but you can
remind people of the past and I think we have to, in an accurate, real way.
    —*Antoine Fuqua, June 15, 2020*

Dear Gordon or is it Peter?
Today i Googled 'Whipped

Peter' and got 8,230,000 hits
in 0.89 seconds. i found out

Will Smith will be playing you
in an action-thriller called

Emancipation, "based on a
true story fueled by that in-

delible image." i downloaded
the carte de visite from your

Wiki, the abolitionist calling
card still circulating widely in

the public domain. i know
you can't fix the past. i can

only imagine what they'll do
to you with a budget. i have

no use for Nostalgia, but i am
your descendent, here to re-

mind you of the past, to make
you whole. i want you to know i Photo-

shopped your back, removed
each tally mark with the Eraser

Tool, restored your skin with the
Clone Stamp, and touched you up

with the Healing Brush. i combed
your hair and oiled your scalp and

rubbed a little coco butter on your
shoulders. A little salve or a bit of

salvation, i pray I've done you no
harm. May that all signifying star,

the untethered keloid of our mean
remembering, find a new sky and

hold its place in a kinder loving uni-

verse. May you carry a lighter burden,
if only for a little while, and find some

relief from a lifetime of Februaries.

Siki

nothin fake about wrestling

nothin fake about coming thru
the back door to go to work

nothin fake about my flash my flare
my white teeth

my cape my shorts
my white boots

my glitter my sequins
my bleach-blond hair

nothin fake about these
big black arms locked round
my white opponent

nothin fake about these
big black arms wrapped round
my beautiful white wife

nothin fake about this black skin
and those pointy white hoods waiting
in the front row

nothin fake about wrestling

nothing fake about the chokehold
I just didn't need it

(there are more skillful ways
to take a man down)

nothin fake about white folks
paying to see you win in the ring
—praying you'll lose outside

nothin fake about my shuffle step
and that little somethin-somethin on the end
of my drop kick

Black Heroin(e)

for Gwen Miller

R_x	
	Name: _____ Date: _____
Prescription:	**RollerGames: Gwen Miller (Skinny Minnie) Video Tribute** 56, 436 views • Feb 18, 2011 Watch 3:35 to 3:46 for when you don't like to be pushed on Repeat: **TAKE DAILY AS NEEDED**

Fair Use

An intention forms the basis of all communication, but this intention must be sincere. In order to discover and desire that sincerity, a distinction must be made between the world and the sum of objects to be found on the earth. Faced with objects, we act differently then when we are faced with people.
—*Frantz Fanon*

With everything we do, we will make it clear that our Black employees matter, Black Pinners and creators matter, and Black Lives Matter. —*Ben Silbermann*

The oppressed and the exploited of the earth maintain their defiance: liberty from theft. —*Ngũgĩ wa Thiong'o*

Dear Ben S   June 2, 2020

As you work to ensure the Pinterest content represents people from diverse backgrounds, I strongly advise you begin the work of unlearning by removing all representations and references to me by way of writing or visual image, including, but not limited to:

- dolls
- figurines
- cookie jars
- measuring cups
- measuring spoons
- egg timers
- salt n pepper shakers
- coffee tins
- tea pots
- creamers
- sugar bowls
- cups
- saucers
- spice jars
- canister sets
- syrup dispensers
- knife holders
- toaster covers
- paper towel holders
- tea towels
- napkins
- toothpick holders
- table cloths
- potholders
- placemats
- plates
- toilet roll holders
- soap dish
- laundry bags
- laundry baskets
- washin' powder
- clothes pin dolls
- wall clocks
- tape measures
- embroidery transfers
- clothes brushes
- note pads
- wooden grocery lists
- wall pockets
- match holders
- coin banks
- ceramic planters
- broom dolls
- door stops

As a non-historical figure, an unlived ghost—a fabrication of the colonial cultural imagination—I do not actually exist. I'm a phantom of the racist imagination. Let's face it, no one smiles that much. I am the product of a capitalist economy driven by false nostalgia and an insatiable need for instant pancakes. Sorry to get all bell hooks and ruin the good times, but I never cooked white people breakfast and I sure as sugar never wasted a tear on their kids. Despite the current social climate, with all the hashtags and decolonising, there's been a fetishizing rise in my currency and an algorithmic shift in my market value. So, where's my cut? Where's my royalty check? Ironic isn't it? Just because I don't exist, don't mean I don't matter. I am no empty signifier. Ask any Black Pinner who ever had to look at me grinning from the center of a dining table—if she don't flinch, she got a bad bad case of Memorabilia. So while you're reflecting and educating yourself, consulting outside experts, type Mammy or Mammie into the search bar, see where it leads you. Watch out for the Gollywogs, Golliwogs, Sambos and Tar Babies, Coons, Jemimas, Mingos, Darkies and lantern carrying Lawn Jockies—they'll be next. I'm holding you to your promise. Your non-compliance may result in a class action.

Mammy

20/20

(for Chelsea)

Not enough light said the message on her screen. She stood in front of the window with no luck. She brought over a lamp, and when one lamp wouldn't suffice, she brought in a second.

—*Globe and Mail, December 16, 2020*

Not enough light?

Little Sister
they see you now

You've corrupted centuries
of programming

Somewhere there's a riot
of ERROR messages

illuminating
their artificial

intelligence.

Little Sister
they see you now

You've corrupted centuries
of programming

Somewhere an ancestor
walking alone at night

has blown out a lantern
and said

good night.

Add Hominem
(sculpting the face of my ancestor)

wrap clay around the base

for a strong foundation

add more than you think you need

to thicken the neck then add

more and more and more

hammer the skull with your fists to release the air

score a line across the face to mark the horizon

add the eyes, lightly gouge them to sleep

smooth away the wrinkle in the brow

rub your thumbs gently over the cheeks

unclench the teeth   release the jaw

erase the parentheses around the mouth

Finding My Roots

If all that's left is Science
let's skip the 14-day free

trial and the $129 start-up
fee. i have read and agree

to the <u>Terms n Conditions</u>.

If all that's left is Science
let's skip the prime-time

reality show, let's skip the
sympathetic host, let's skip

the establishing shot and
the empty family tree.

If all that's left is Science,
let's skip the Getty images

and the choir humming in
the background. Let's skip

the big reveal, the dramatic
page turn, the hands over

mouth, the gaping cesura,
the close up, the look away,

the welling eyes, the hold.
Let's skip the *I told myself*

I wouldn't cry and get off
this celebrity trope train.

GO BACK

**to where
you came from**

If all that's left is Science,
let's skip to the end and

cut to my conclusion. Let
me stand at the shore of

these shattered days. Let
me wade neck-deep into

the middle of this viscous
wound and tread in the un-

known. Let me lean back
and listen to my pumping

blood-rattle telling me i am
a beloved child of the first

mother, kin n cousin to
Lupita, that some tiny part

of me existed when the world
was Black, that my people

were poets, artists, shaman,
schemers, philosophers

musicians, gamblers, whores,
that i have a direct line to

the horizon, that i am held
in the wake of my ancestors,

my every cell fitted with a pen,
a knife, and an oxygen mask.

**BE A GOOD
ANCESTOR**

TODAY

Bye Bye, Wakanda

because they can't imagine us
in the future

because they can't see us un-
tethered
from   the past

because the thought of us with-
out them   unravels
their DNA

because they still run
from a single
drop of
blood

because they measure space
with a straight
ruler

because they measure time
with circular
three-fisted clocks

because they make every second
count

1 Mississippi, 2 Mississippi

because their tools are out-
dated

because their means are un-
civilized

because we're indentured
to a life
of dozens

because they've banked
on our fear

because they've invested
in our suffering

because we are always
their bottom
line

because we count
in the 12
millions

because they can only love us
one
at a time

In Lieu of Flowers

In lieu of flowers clear your history

In lieu of flowers disable comments

In lieu of flowers turn off notifications

In lieu of flowers switch to silent

In lieu of flowers

exhale

hold...

inhale

The Bottom Line

NOTHING INSIDE IS WORTH DYING FOR NOTHING INSIDE IS
WORTH DYING FOR NOTHING INSIDE IS WORTH DYING FOR
NOTHING INSIDE IS WORTH DYING FOR NOTHING INSIDE IS
WORTH DYING FOR NOTHING INSIDE IS WORTH DYING FOR
NOTHING INSIDE IS WORTH DYING FOR NOTHING INSIDE IS
WORTH DYING FOR NOTHING INSIDE IS WORTH DYING FOR
NOTHING INSIDE IS WORTH DYING FOR NOTHING INSIDE IS
WORTH DYING FOR NOTHING INSIDE IS WORTH DYING FOR
NOTHING INSIDE IS WORTH DYING FOR NOTHING INSIDE IS
WORTH DYING FOR NOTHING INSIDE IS WORTH DYING FOR
NOTHING INSIDE IS WORTH DYING FOR NOTHING INSIDE IS
WORTH DYING FOR NOTHING INSIDE IS WORTH DYING FOR

Acknowledgments

With thanks and gratitude:

To my poetry editor Chelene Knight for your nuanced care and attention to this work and to our readers.

To my graphics editor and dope ally Andrew Hawryshkewich for listening and asking and listening and...

To the folks at Caitlin Press, my thanks to Vici Johnstone for saying yes to this project from the start—for giving me this generous space to do my work, for respecting my practice, and for supporting me with the resources to do it. With gratitude for every image tweak, font change, line break, space, nudge and letter *i*.

And my thanks to Sarah Corsie and Malaika Aleba for your excellent work behind the scenes and in the quiet corners of this book.

To Dionne Brand, bell hooks, Lawrence Hill, Audre Lorde, Toni Morrison, M. NourbeSe Philip, Saidiya Hartman, Christina Sharpe, Ngũgĩ wa Thiong'o and Frantz Fanon—whose work and words have made room for mine.

To Otoniya J. Okot Bitek, Canisia Lubrin, Ebony Magnus, Fiona Tinwei Lam, Andrew Thomas Hunter, David Chariandy, Hannah McGregor, Baharak Yousefi, Hazel Jane Plante, Onjana Yawnghwe, Kate Hennessy, Gabriela Aceves-Sepúlveda, Alissa Antle, Thecla Schiphorst, Kevin Stewart, Stephanie Dayes, and Carman Neustaedter for your generous support.

To James Phillips, for every Black book you ever gave me.

To my colleagues and students

To my family and friends

To Bruce, my love

To Julie, my yellow love

To Joan, my witness

To my readers

To our ancestors

To us.

Notes:

Cover image: Digitally altered photo from *Dangling Modifiers*, 2019, mixed media video installation by Chantal Gibson (artist) and Adrian Bisek (videographer).

p.8: "hand wash cold" graphic poem inspired by a partially revealed bra tag captured in Exhibit 47 crime scene photo as presented in *The New York Times* "How the Police Killed Breonna Taylor Visual Investigations" (December 28, 2020). https://www.youtube.com/watch?v=lDaNU7yDnsc

p.10: Epigraph is from Frantz Fanon's *The Wretched of the Earth* (New York: Grove, 2004), 182.

p.12: "Add to Cart" was informed by my research on the accessibility and instant makeability of racial, racialized and racist objects on a range of Canadian and American DIY art design and merch sites. What began with me checking-out an artist friend's product line (thanks JB) turned into a fascination with TAGS, search terms, digital artifacts and a wide range of consumer surfaces.

p.22: "whitewash (under lying messages)" is a response to a wide range of 2020 solidarity statements from consumer driven companies, corporations, and social media platforms in response to the murder of George Floyd on May 25, 2020 and the #BlackLivesMatter movement.

p.26: "Blackfish" is a response to the online article "TikTok Star Addison Rae Accused of Blackfishing. What is Blackfishing?" (CBC Kids News, July 8, 2020) and news stories related to Rachel Dolezal (2015) and Jessica Krug (2020), both white women falsely claiming Black heritage and making a living as academics teaching Black Studies.

p.66: white wink icon courtesy of iconsdb.com https://www.iconsdb.com/white-icons/wink-icon.html

p.92: Epigraph is from Frantz Fanon's *The Psychiatric Writings from Alienation and Freedom* (New York: Bloomsbury Academic, 2021), 121. Translated by Steven Corcoran.

p.93: The term *"Journal de bord"* is borrowed directly from the entry "24 December 1953, no. 1. Memory and journal" in Fanon's *The Psychiatric Readings* translated by Steven Corcoran. Fanon references the ship as the state of being "cut off from the world." To remedy this disconnection, Fanon discusses the publication of a journal by and for ward patients. A proponent of social therapy, Fanon believed that patient engagement with regular news and images from the outside, including arts, film, music and recreation, would help ease feelings of disconnection and isolation (p. 155). Fanon encouraged writing and creative thinking, supporting patient-run film, music and cultural clubs.

During 2020-21 Covid-19 lockdown, this book became my own Journal de bord/ late-night boredom journal as I struggled with my own feelings of isolation and disconnection in the daily onslaught of bad news: the murders of Black men, women and kids at the hands of law enforcement, assaults on Indigenous people, Brown people, Asian people, and other People of Colour, attacks on LGBTQ2+ folk, and the insidious undermining of science and gaslighting of human intelligence. While I had come to know Fanon the Revolutionary in grad school, I was moved by *Dr. Fanon*, his focus on humanity, the role of culture in meaning-making and his belief in the temporariness of the ship—the possibility that his patients/passengers could eventually reconnect with loved ones and "return home" (p. 155).

p.97: "Rotten Tomato" epigraph is from bell hooks' *Teaching to Transgress: Education as the Practice of Freedom* (New York: Routledge, 1994), 67. The poem is in response to the February 8, 2018 social media backlash that occurred when the film *Black Panther* was given its first negative review, ruining the 100% rating on *Rotten Tomatoes*.

p.99: Plaque text is cited from the Simon Fraser (1776-1862) statue at New Westminster Quay Market. Constructed in 1908, it was moved to this riverside location in 1988. Note: Simon Fraser University has campuses in Vancouver, Burnaby and Surrey, British Columbia. Surrey campus architect Bing Thom was mentored by Burnaby campus architect Arthur Erickson.

p.99: "Ad Hominem" epigraph is from Ngũgĩ wa Thiong'o's *Decolonising the Mind, The Politics of Language in African Literature* (USA: Heinemann, 2011). First published in 1986.

p.107: "Old Souls" epigraph is from Frantz Fanon's *Black Skin, White Masks* (New York: Grove, 2008), 123.

p.112: "Other Ways of Knowing, Expo 67" brings together 1930s African fine art and 1970s North American professional wrestling and Canadian monuments such as an Arthur Erickson and his iconic buildings and the mythologized *Bluenose II*, a memorialising replica of the *Bluenose I* racing schooner that sunk off the coast of Haiti in 1946. These cultural texts can be seen, in the Ngũgĩ wa Thiong'o sense, as different expressions of the colonial condition, teaching us something about what it means to locate, place, and center Black bodies and Black creative and intellectual thought inside systemically white spaces. Only through an Expo '67 promotional video on YouTube did I encounter for the first time the work of Papa Ibra Tall inside the Erickson pavilion. A google search of Ibra Tall led me to Senegalese poet Léopold Sédar Senghor and the 1930s Négritude movement, founded by Martinican poet Aimé Césaire who influenced Fanon, who influenced Ngũgĩ, who...

p.117: "Trolling Cape Coast Castle" was inspired by my first encounter with the work of Ghanaian artist Kwame Akoto-Bamfo whose *Ancestor Project* uses the Akan tradition of sculpting portraits of the dead to express the myriad reactions to and experiences of capture as Africans approached enslavement castles. I found this installation of many voices compelling, jarring and disrupting—juxtaposed against the singular narrative of the tour guides. https://www.bbc.com/news/av/world-africa-48744703

p.122: "Forensic Report" responds to my four-month analysis of *The New York Times* "How the Police Killed Breonna Taylor Visual Investigations" (December 28, 2020). As we neared the end of a-year-without-ending, I got pinged and started exploring the objects inside the documents, thinking about this slick seamless remediated journalism, the many stories it was telling, thinking about a chat with Canisia Lubrin and the stories I was telling, thinking about Saidiya Hartman's *Lose Your Mother* and my role as a reader-witness-tourist. As I watched the view count approach one million, I wondered who else had watched this video. I wondered how they watched—and how they were changed afterward. https://www.youtube.com/watch?v=lDaNU7yDnsc

p.129: Plaque excerpt is from the "Foot Soldier" statue in Birmingham's Kelly Ingram Park designed by artist Ronald McDowell, dedication by mayor Richard Arrington, Jr. in 1995.

p.129: "Revisionist History" is inspired by Malcolm Gladwell's podcast series of the same name, Season 2, Episode "The Foot Soldier of Birmingham: Oh, Mac. What did you do?" https://www.pushkin.fm/show/revisionist-history/

p.131: "Fanon's Couch" epigraph is from Frantz Fanon *Black Skin, White Masks* (New York: Grove, 2008), 99.

p.131: In "Fanon's Couch" the quote that begins "way grudgingly and insecurely..." is borrowed from Dionne Brand's poem "Forgetting 9" in *A Map to the Door of No Return: Notes to Belonging* (Canada: Vintage, 2011), 28.

p.134: In "Fanon's Couch" the quote "not enough light" is borrowed from "Use of surveillance software to crack down on exam cheating has unintended consequences" by Joe Friesen in the *Globe and Mail* December 16, 2020 https://www.theglobeandmail.com/canada/article-use-of-surveillance-software-to-crack-down-on-exam-cheating-has/

p.135: In "Fanon's Couch" the quote "offending human dignity" is borrowed from "A French tempest in a breakfast cup" by Mary Blume in T*he New York*

Times February 16, 2006 https://www.nytimes.com/2006/02/16/arts/a-french-tempest-in-a-breakfast-cup.html

p.136: In "Fanon's Couch" the reference to artist Willie Cole's ironing board woodcut print entitled Stowage, 1997 in the Whitney Museum of American Art. https://whitney.org/collection/works/11661

p.136: In "Fanon's Couch" the reference to a South African company's use of slave ship imagery on ironing boards comes from "The Slave Ship Theme" by Africa Is a Country in AfricasaCountry.com.
https://africasacountry.com/2014/04/maid-in-africa-the-cape-town-company-that-designs-a-slave-ship-ironing-board

p.138: In "Fanon's Couch" the reference to the Gollywog page on Pinterest https://www.pinterest.ca/search/pins/?q=gollywog&rs=typo_auto_origi-nal&auto_correction_disabled=true

p.141: In "Fanon's Couch" the reference to the BBC News article is from "Manet, Picasso and Cezanne works renamed after Black models" March 26, 2019 https://www.bbc.com/news/entertainment-arts-47705284

p.142: In "Fanon's Couch" the reference to slavery yoga is from "Slavery Yoga was Taught to Kindergarteners in Delaware" by Jack Lindly in *The Root* February 28, 2021 https://www.theroot.com/slavery-yoga-was-taught-to-kindergarten-ers-in-delaware-1846376305

p.146: Epigraph from bell hooks' *Teaching to Transgress: Education as the Practice of Freedom* (New York: Routledge, 1994), 61.

p.148: "unmasking Nostalgia" borrows from https://en.wikipedia.org/wiki/Nostalgia.

p.152: "State Sanctioned Violence" is a response to widespread media coverage of photographs of Justin Trudeau in blackface: "Justin Trudeau Wore Brownface at 2001 'Arabian Nights' Party While He Taught at a Private School" by Anna Purna Kambhampaty, Madeleine Carlisle, Melissa Chan in *TIME* September 19, 2019 https://time.com/5680759/justin-trudeau-brownface-photo/.
"What we know about Justin Trudeau's blackface photos—and what happens next." CBC News September 26, 2019 https://www.cbc.ca/news/politics/cana-da-votes-2019-trudeau-blackface-brownface-cbc-explains-1.5290664.
In satirist Sacha Baron Cohen's October 2020 film *Borat Subsequent Moviefilm*, directed by Jason Woliner.

p.153: "The Punctum Suite: How to Bear Witness, Notes from Mamie Till-Mob-ley" honours Mamie Till-Mobley teacher, educator, activist and beloved mother of Emmett Till.

p.155: In "The Punctum Suite: Care Instructions" epigraph is from "Mamie-Mobley dies, 81, Dies; Son, Emmett, Slain in 1955" by John W. Fountain in The *New York Times*, January 7, 2003. https://www.nytimes.com/2003/01/07/us/mamie-mobley-81-dies-son-emmett-till-slain-in-1955.html

p.157: "EMT (Emancipation Modification Therapy)" epigraph and reference to upcoming film is from "Antoine Fuqua & Will Smith Runaway Slave Thriller 'Emancipation' To Be Introduced At Virtual Cannes Market; Based On Indelible 'Scourged Back' Photo" by Mike Fleming in *Deadline*, June 15, 2020. https://deadline.com/2020/06/antoine-fuqua-will-smith-emancipation-runaway-slave-movie-package-the-scourged-back-photo-timely-virtual-cannes-market-title-1202959110/

p.157: "EMT (Emancipation Modification Therapy)" reference to the iconic status of the Gordon photograph is from Silkenat, D. 2014, '"A Typical Negro": Gordon, Peter, Vincent Colyer, and the story behind slavery's most famous photograph,' American Nineteenth Century History, vol. 15, no. 2, pp. 169-186. https://doi.org/10.1080/14664658.2014.939807

p.159: To "Sweet Daddy Siki" with gratitude for the drop-kick. See "Sweet Daddy Siki" 2017 documentary directed by Harvey Glazer.

p.161: "Black Heroin(e)" is an ode to Gwen "Skinny Minnie" Miller (September 12, 1951 – May 7, 2018) based on her quote "I don't like to fight, but then, too, I don't like to be pushed on…Sometimes you will get these skaters that will taunt you. …if they know you're a pushover, they'll keep at you. The next thing you know, you are a pushover. You have to defend yourself, just like in life." posted on Rolla Skate Club facebook page post June 5, 2020 and the dopest 10 seconds in roller derby. If only I could put a link in this page! Rollergames: Gwen Miller (Skinny Minnie) Miller Video Tribute Retrieved: https://www.youtube.com/watch?v=Fdc9efl1tA8&t=222s

p.162: "Fair Use" is a response to "Listening and Acting" the Pinterest Black Lives Matter Statement posted June 2, 2020 by co-founder and CEO Ben Silbermann. https://newsroom.pinterest.com/en/post/listening-and-acting

p.162: "Fair Use" epigraph 1 is from Frantz Fanon's *The Psychiatric Writings from Alienation and Freedom* (New York: Bloomsbury Academic, 2021), 121; epigraph 2 is from "Listening and Acting" the Pinterest Black Lives Matter Statement posted June 2, 2020 by co-founder and CEO Ben Silbermann. https://newsroom.pinterest.com/en/post/listening-and-acting; epigraph 3 is from Ngũgĩ wa Thiong'o's *Decolonising the Mind, The Politics of Language in African Literature*. (USA: Heinemann, 2011), 3.

p.162: The extensive list of Mammy memorabilia in the poem was derived searching for and cross-listing items noted in Patricia Turner's *Ceramic Uncles*

& Celluloid Mammie: Black Images and Their Influence on Black Culture (New York: Anchor, 1994).

p.164: "20/20" is a response to "Use of Surveillance software to crack down on exam cheating has unintended consequences" by Joe Friesen in *The Globe and Mail* December 16, 2020 and to Chelsea Okankwu, a Concordia student whose story and image made the front page of my classroom in 2021. https://www.theglobeandmail.com/canada/article-use-of-surveillance-software-to-crack-down-on-exam-cheating-has/

p.164: "20/20" reference to US Lantern Laws was informed by Dr. Cecelia Parthner (St. John's University) and Dr. Sarah Elain Eaton (University of Calgary) *Student Perspectives on the Impact of Race in Educational Surveillance and Proctoring Technologies*, International Center for Academic Integrity Conference, March 2, 2021.

p.165: "Add Hominem" is inspired by Ghanaian artist Kwame Akoto-Bamfo whose work taught me about Nsodie the Akan tradition of memorializing sculpture and by African American poet A Van Jordan's poem "Sculpting the Head of Miles Davis" in *Quantum Lyrics* (New York: Norton 2007), 99.

p.168: "Bye Bye, Wakanda" was inspired by LA Clipper coach Doc Rivers tearful, post-game response to the shooting of Jacob Blake August 23, 2020. "It's amazing why we keep loving this country, and this country does not love us back...It's really so sad. Like, I should just be a coach. I'm so often reminded of my color. It's just really sad. We got to do better. But we got to demand better." https://nba.nbcsports.com/2020/08/26/doc-rivers-we-keep-loving-this-country-and-this-country-does-not-love-us-back/

p.172: "The Bottom Line" is inspired by a neighbour's front door mat in crime scene photos from *The New York Times* "How the Police Killed Breonna Taylor Visual Investigations" (December 28, 2020).

Selected Readings:

Brand, Dionne. *A Map to the Door of No Return: Notes to Belonging* (Canada: Vintage, 2011).

Brand, Dionne. *The Blue Clerk* (Toronto: McClelland & Stewart, 2019).

Fanon, Frantz. *The Psychiatric Writings from Alienation and Freedom* (New York: Bloomsbury Academic, 2021).

Fanon, Frantz. *Black Skin, White Masks* (New York: Grove, 2008).

Fanon, Frantz. *The Wretched of the Earth* (New York: Grove, 2004).

Hartman, Saidiya. *Lose Your Mother, A Journey Along the Atlantic Slave Route* (New York: Farrar, Straus and Giroux, 2007).

hooks, bell. *Teaching to Transgress: Education as the Practice of Freedom* (New York: Routledge, 1994).

Philip, M. NourbeSe. *Zong!* (Toronto: Mercury Press, 2008).

Sharpe, Christina. *In the Wake: On Blackness and Being* (Duke: Durham, 2016).

Thiong'o, Ngũgĩ wa. *Decolonising the Mind, The Politics of Language in African Literature* (USA: Heinemann, 2011).

Turner, Patricia. *Ceramic Uncles & Celluloid Mammie: Black Images and Their Influence on Black Culture* (New York: Anchor, 1994).

Chantal Gibson is an award-winning writer-artist-educator living on the unceded, traditional, ancestral lands of the Coast Salish Peoples. Working in the overlap between literary and visual art, her work confronts colonialism head on, imagining the BIPOC voices silenced in the spaces and omissions left by systemic cultural and institutional erasure. Her visual art has been exhibited in museums and galleries across Canada and the US, most recently in the Senate of Canada building in Ottawa.

Gibson's debut book of poetry, *How She Read* (Caitlin Press, 2019), was the winner of the 2020 Pat Lowther Memorial Award and the Dorothy Livesay Poetry Prize, a finalist for both the 2020 Griffin Poetry Prize and the inaugural Jim Deva Prize for Writing That Provokes. *How She Read* received second place for the Fred Cogswell Award for Excellence in Poetry, and was longlisted for the Nelson Ball Poetry Prize, the Gerald Lampert Memorial Award, and the Raymond Souster Award. Gibson's work has been published in *Canadian Art*, *The Capilano Review*, *The Literary Review of Canada*, *Room* magazine and *Making Room: 40 years of Room Magazine* (Caitlin Press, 2017) and was longlisted for the 2020 CBC Poetry prize.

Recipient of the prestigious 2021 3M National Teaching Fellowship, Gibson teaches writing and visual communication in the School of Interactive Arts & Technology at Simon Fraser University.